AI-Powered Cyber Defense Systems

Using Artificial Intelligence to Detect, Block & Stop Cyber Threats

By Joe Correa

Published by Live Stronger Faster

First Edition

Table of Contents

Introduction

In the modern digital battlefield, speed is everything. Cyberattacks no longer unfold over days or even hours; they happen in milliseconds, faster than any human analyst can react. Malware now rewrites itself in real time, phishing campaigns adapt on the fly, and automated bots probe millions of systems simultaneously looking for microscopic weaknesses. This reality has rendered traditional cybersecurity models dangerously obsolete. Firewalls, antivirus software, and static rulesets were built for a slower era—one in which threats were predictable, signatures could be cataloged, and human teams had time to investigate alerts before damage occurred. Today's attackers are not just people sitting behind keyboards; they are algorithms, autonomous agents, and AI-powered attack engines designed to learn, evolve, and strike at machine speed. This is why AI-powered cyber defense systems are no longer optional. They are the only viable way to survive in an environment where machines are attacking machines.

AI-driven cybersecurity represents a fundamental shift in how digital defense works. Instead of reacting to known threats after they have already caused harm, AI systems operate by continuously analyzing behavior, predicting risk, and stopping attacks before they succeed. They do not wait for malware signatures to be added to a database or for a security team to write new rules. They learn what "normal" looks like inside a network, on a device, or across a cloud environment, and then instantly identify anything that deviates from that baseline. A user logging in from an unusual location, a server suddenly sending data to a foreign IP address, or a program attempting to escalate privileges without authorization can all be flagged and neutralized in real time. This predictive, self-learning approach transforms cybersecurity from a slow, reactive process into a living, adaptive defense system.

The reason AI cyber defense is so powerful lies in its ability to process massive volumes of data at once. Modern organizations generate billions of security-relevant events every day: logins, file transfers, API calls, email messages, database queries, device connections, and more. No human team could possibly review this data fast enough to detect subtle attack patterns hidden within it. AI systems, however, thrive on complexity. They ingest data from every corner of the digital ecosystem, correlate it across systems, and discover relationships that would otherwise remain invisible. A single phishing email, when viewed alone, might look harmless. But when AI sees that the same message triggered credential theft, unusual logins, and abnormal financial transactions across hundreds of users, it instantly identifies an active attack campaign and moves to shut it down.

Another critical advantage of AI-powered defense systems is their ability to adapt to new and unknown threats. Traditional security tools depend heavily on predefined rules and known attack signatures, which makes them vulnerable to zero-day exploits, polymorphic malware, and novel hacking techniques. AI, on the other hand, does not need to recognize a specific piece of malware to know something is wrong. It evaluates behavior instead of relying solely on fingerprints. If a piece of software suddenly begins encrypting large numbers of files, communicating with command-and-control servers, or disabling security controls, an AI system will recognize this as malicious—even if the malware has never been seen before. This ability to stop threats based on intent rather than identity is what makes AI cyber defense uniquely suited for the modern threat landscape.

AI also transforms how cybersecurity teams operate. In traditional environments, security analysts are overwhelmed by alerts—many of which are false positives. Teams waste enormous amounts of time chasing benign anomalies while real attacks slip through unnoticed. AI reduces this noise by prioritizing threats based on risk, context, and likelihood of damage. It can tell the difference between a harmless system update and a coordinated breach attempt, allowing human experts to focus on the most dangerous situations. In this way, AI does not replace security professionals; it amplifies their effectiveness, turning small teams into powerful cyber defense units capable of protecting massive digital infrastructures.

As organizations increasingly move their operations to the cloud, AI becomes even more essential. Cloud environments are highly dynamic: servers are spun up and shut down automatically, workloads shift between regions, and users access systems from all over the world. Static security controls struggle to keep up with this constant change. AI-powered systems, however, are designed for dynamic environments. They continuously learn the evolving structure of the network, the behavior of users, and the flow of data, adjusting their models in real time. This allows them to protect modern cloud-based businesses, financial platforms, healthcare systems, and government networks with a level of precision that traditional tools cannot achieve.

The stakes of cyber defense have never been higher. AI-driven attacks are now capable of targeting power grids, financial markets, hospitals, military systems, and even democratic institutions. A single successful breach can disrupt entire economies, shut down critical infrastructure, or expose the private data of millions of people. In this context, AI-powered cyber defense systems are not just tools for IT departments—they are pillars of national security, economic stability, and public safety. Governments and corporations alike are racing to deploy intelligent defense platforms that can detect and neutralize threats before they escalate into full-scale digital disasters.

This book will take you inside the world of AI-powered cyber defense, showing you how these systems work, why they are so effective, and how they are reshaping the future of cybersecurity. You will learn how machine learning models detect anomalies, how neural networks identify malicious behavior, how automated response systems stop attacks in real time, and how organizations can deploy AI to protect networks, applications, endpoints, and cloud infrastructure. Whether you are a cybersecurity professional, a business leader, a government policymaker, or simply someone who wants to understand how the digital world is being defended, this book will give you a clear, practical, and deeply insightful view of the most powerful security technology ever created.

In the war between attackers and defenders, AI has become the ultimate force multiplier. Just as hackers use artificial intelligence to automate, scale, and refine their attacks, defenders now use AI to outthink, outpace, and overpower those threats. The future of cybersecurity will not be decided by who has the largest team or the most expensive software—it will be decided by who has the smartest, fastest, and most adaptive AI. AI-powered cyber defense systems are the shield that stands between civilization and chaos in the digital age. This book will show you how that shield is built, how it works, and how it will shape the future of global security.

Chapter 1

The Rise of AI-Powered Cyber Defense

The digital world has entered a new era of warfare, one where battles are no longer fought with missiles, tanks, or soldiers but with data, algorithms, and autonomous code. Every device connected to the internet—phones, laptops, servers, cars, medical equipment, financial systems—has become a potential battlefield. In this environment, cyberattacks are not isolated crimes but continuous, automated campaigns driven by artificial intelligence. Hackers no longer need to manually scan networks or write custom exploits for every target. Instead, they deploy AI systems that can test millions of vulnerabilities, mimic human behavior, and adapt their tactics in real time. This has created a situation in which traditional cybersecurity defenses are overwhelmed by the sheer speed, scale, and intelligence of modern attacks.

AI-powered cyber defense emerged as a direct response to this new threat landscape. Unlike conventional security tools that rely on static rules and known signatures, AI systems learn from data. They observe how users log in, how applications communicate, how files move, and how systems normally behave. Over time, these models create a living map of what "normal" looks like inside an organization's digital ecosystem.

When something unusual occurs—such as a sudden spike in data transfers, an abnormal login pattern, or a strange program execution—the AI recognizes it as a potential threat. This allows security systems to detect attacks that would otherwise go unnoticed until it is too late.

One of the most powerful aspects of AI cyber defense is its ability to detect previously unknown threats. Many of the most dangerous attacks today are zero-day exploits, meaning they take advantage of vulnerabilities that no one has discovered or patched yet. Traditional antivirus software is nearly useless against these attacks because it cannot recognize what it has never seen. AI, however, does not need a known signature. It analyzes behavior instead. If a program begins performing actions that resemble malicious intent—such as encrypting files, modifying system settings, or contacting suspicious servers—the AI can intervene immediately. This behavioral approach allows organizations to stop attacks even when the malware itself is completely new.

AI-powered defense systems also bring unprecedented speed to cybersecurity. Human analysts may take minutes or hours to investigate an alert, but in a modern cyberattack, those minutes are enough for attackers to steal data, deploy ransomware, or take control of entire networks. AI systems respond in milliseconds. They can automatically isolate infected devices, block malicious traffic, disable compromised accounts, and roll back harmful changes before serious damage occurs. This ability to act instantly is what transforms AI from a detection tool into a true defense system.

Another key advantage of AI cyber defense is its ability to operate across massive, complex environments. Modern organizations often run thousands of servers, cloud platforms, remote devices, and third-party services, all connected through intricate networks. Monitoring this environment manually is impossible. AI systems, however, thrive in complexity. They continuously ingest data from every part of the infrastructure, correlating events across systems and identifying patterns that humans would never see. A single login from a suspicious IP address might not trigger an alarm on its own, but when combined with unusual data access and network activity, AI can recognize a coordinated attack.

AI also plays a critical role in defending against social engineering and identity-based attacks. Many cyber breaches begin not with technical exploits but with tricking users into revealing passwords, clicking malicious links, or approving fraudulent transactions. AI-powered security systems analyze communication patterns, writing styles, and behavioral signals to detect phishing emails, fake messages, and deepfake scams. They can identify when an email that appears to come from a

CEO or financial officer does not match that person's usual tone, timing, or behavior. This adds a powerful layer of protection against the most common and dangerous form of cybercrime.

As cyber threats continue to evolve, AI cyber defense systems are becoming more autonomous. In the past, security tools simply raised alarms and waited for humans to respond. Today's AI-driven platforms are capable of taking action on their own, making risk-based decisions in real time. They can block traffic, quarantine files, revoke access, and even reconfigure network defenses automatically. This level of automation is essential in an era where attacks happen too fast for human intervention. The goal is not to remove humans from cybersecurity, but to ensure that AI handles the immediate response while humans focus on strategy, investigation, and recovery.

The rise of AI-powered cyber defense represents a shift from reactive security to proactive protection. Instead of waiting for attacks to succeed and then cleaning up the damage, organizations can now identify threats at the earliest stages and stop them before they cause harm. This approach not only reduces financial losses and downtime but also protects customer trust, national security, and the integrity of digital systems. In a world where data is one of the most valuable resources, AI cyber defense is the guardian that keeps it safe.

This new generation of cybersecurity technology is not limited to large corporations or governments. Cloud-based AI security platforms are making advanced protection accessible to small businesses, hospitals, schools, and individuals. As more of life moves online, from banking and healthcare to communication and entertainment, everyone becomes a stakeholder in digital security. AI-powered defense systems ensure that protection scales alongside risk, making it possible to defend even the most complex digital environments.

The future of cybersecurity belongs to artificial intelligence. Attackers are already using AI to automate hacking, generate convincing scams, and evade detection. Defenders must meet that challenge with equally intelligent systems. AI-powered cyber defense is not just an upgrade to existing tools—it is a complete transformation of how security works. It is the difference between being constantly under siege and having a shield that adapts, learns, and fights back on your behalf.

"The Network That Fought Back"

When Maya Alvarez logged into the security operations center at dawn, the wall of monitors in front of her looked calm, almost peaceful. Data flowed across the screens in quiet streams of green and blue, each line representing millions of digital interactions happening every second across the global network her company protected. To most people, it would look like abstract art, but to Maya, it was a living organism—one that could be wounded if not carefully watched. What made this network different from any she had worked on before was its brain: an AI-powered defense system that never slept, never blinked, and never got tired.

At first, the attack was invisible. No alarms blared. No systems crashed. But the AI noticed something subtle: a series of login attempts coming from devices that behaved just slightly differently from normal users. They typed too fast, moved too smoothly, and accessed data in patterns that didn't quite match any known employee. The AI flagged the behavior, not because it matched a known threat, but because it didn't belong. Within milliseconds, it began quietly tracking the activity, building a profile of the intruder as it moved through the network.

Maya watched as the AI's confidence score rose. The system began to see the shape of the attack—a swarm of AI-powered bots designed to steal financial records and customer identities. In the past, this kind of intrusion might have taken hours to detect. Now, it took seconds. Without waiting for human approval, the AI isolated the affected systems, cutting off the attackers' access while allowing legitimate users to continue working. To the outside world, nothing seemed wrong. Inside the digital battlefield, however, a war was unfolding.

The attackers tried to adapt. Their bots shifted tactics, attempting to disguise themselves as legitimate services. But the defense AI was learning too. It analyzed every move, updating its models in real time. When the bots tried to reroute through a different server, the AI anticipated the move and blocked the path before the attack could spread. It was like watching two intelligent organisms playing a high-speed game of chess, each move happening faster than any human could follow.

Maya felt a strange mix of awe and relief. Years ago, she had been part of teams that spent nights scrambling to contain breaches, watching helplessly as data was stolen and systems were locked by ransomware. Now, she was witnessing a defense system that didn't just react—it fought back. The AI deployed digital countermeasures, feeding the attackers false data and trapping their bots in a controlled environment where they could do no harm. Every action the intruders took only made them easier to contain.

Within minutes, the attack collapsed. The bots, unable to find any real targets, began to shut down one by one. The AI logged every detail of the encounter, using it to strengthen future defenses. By the time Maya finished her morning coffee, the threat was gone, neutralized so quietly that most of the company never even knew it had existed.

As the sun rose outside the operations center, Maya realized something profound. The network hadn't just been protected—it had protected itself. The AI had become a digital immune system, detecting and eliminating threats the way a body fights off disease. In a world where cyberattacks were growing smarter and more aggressive every day, this was the future: networks that could think, learn, and defend themselves.

Maya leaned back in her chair and smiled. For the first time in her career, she felt that humanity was not losing the cyber war. With AI-powered cyber defense systems standing guard, the digital world finally had a fighting chance.

Chapter 2

How AI Detects Cyber Threats in Real Time

Artificial intelligence does not protect networks the way traditional security software does. Instead of relying on static rules or lists of known malware, AI operates as a constantly learning observer, quietly studying everything that happens across a digital environment. Every login, file transfer, email, application request, and network connection becomes part of a massive data stream that the AI analyzes in real time. Over hours, days, and weeks, it builds a detailed behavioral profile of what is normal for every user, device, and system. This baseline becomes the foundation for threat detection, because in cybersecurity, the most reliable indicator of danger is not a known virus but a deviation from expected behavior.

When something unusual happens, the AI recognizes it instantly. A user logging in from an unexpected location, a server suddenly transferring data at abnormal volumes, or an application attempting to access restricted resources all trigger the system's attention. Unlike traditional tools that might raise thousands of generic alerts, AI evaluates the full context of every event. It looks at time, location, device, historical behavior, and relationships between systems. By understanding the story behind each action, it can determine whether the activity is harmless or potentially malicious. This context-aware detection dramatically reduces false alarms while increasing the chances of catching real attacks.

Machine learning models play a central role in this process. These models are trained on vast datasets containing both normal and malicious behavior. Over time, they learn to distinguish subtle patterns that indicate risk. For example, a piece of malware may try to hide itself by behaving quietly at first, only slowly escalating its actions. A human might not notice anything unusual, but an AI model can detect the slight anomalies in timing, memory usage, or network communication that reveal the presence of an intruder. This allows AI to spot threats long before they cause visible damage.

AI also excels at detecting coordinated attacks. Many cyber intrusions involve multiple components working together, such as phishing emails, compromised accounts, and malicious software. Individually, each of these actions might look normal, but when viewed together, they form a clear attack pattern. AI systems connect these dots automatically, correlating events across different systems and identifying the hidden relationships between them. This holistic view allows organizations to see the full scope of an attack instead of just isolated symptoms.

One of the most powerful aspects of real-time AI detection is its ability to operate continuously without fatigue. Human analysts must sleep, take breaks, and manage workloads, but cyberattacks happen around the clock. AI never stops watching. It processes data at machine speed, ensuring that threats are detected the moment they emerge. This constant vigilance is critical in a world where even a few seconds of delay can be the difference between stopping an attack and suffering a catastrophic breach.

AI systems also learn from every incident they encounter. When a threat is detected and blocked, the details of that event are fed back into the models, making them smarter and more accurate in the future. This creates a powerful feedback loop in which the defense system grows stronger with every attempted attack. Over time, the AI becomes highly specialized to the environment it protects, understanding its unique patterns, workflows, and risks. This adaptability makes it far more effective than one-size-fits-all security tools.

Another important capability of AI threat detection is its ability to handle encrypted and hidden activity. Many modern attacks use encryption to hide malicious traffic, making it difficult for traditional tools to inspect data. AI, however, can analyze metadata, timing, and behavioral patterns even when it cannot see the content itself. It can tell when encrypted traffic behaves in a way that suggests data exfiltration, command-and-control communication, or other malicious activity. This allows organizations to maintain privacy and security at the same time.

Real-time AI detection is also essential for protecting cloud-based and remote work environments. As employees access systems from home, coffee shops, and mobile devices, the attack surface grows exponentially. AI systems track each user's normal behavior across locations and devices, quickly identifying when something does not match. A stolen password alone is no longer enough to break into a system if the AI recognizes that the behavior of the person using it is wrong.

The ultimate goal of AI threat detection is to make cyberattacks visible the moment they begin. Instead of discovering breaches weeks or months after they happen, organizations can now stop them at the door. This proactive approach not only prevents financial losses and data theft but also protects reputations, customer trust, and national security. AI turns cybersecurity into a real-time defense rather than a post-incident investigation.

As cyber threats continue to grow more intelligent and automated, the systems that defend against them must do the same. AI-powered detection is not just an upgrade—it is a fundamental requirement for survival in the digital age. By continuously watching, learning, and adapting, these systems provide a level of awareness that no human team could ever achieve on its own.

"The Moment Before the Breach"

When the first alert appeared on Jonah's dashboard, it didn't look like anything special. Just a tiny flicker in a sea of data, barely noticeable even to a trained eye. But the AI saw it. Somewhere in the sprawling cloud network of a global shipping company, a single login attempt didn't quite fit. It came from a device that had never been used before, at a time when its owner was usually asleep. On its own, it meant nothing. But to the AI, it was the opening note of a dangerous melody.

Jonah leaned forward as the system quietly began to watch. The login was followed by a few cautious clicks, then a file access that didn't match the user's job role. The AI compared these actions to years of historical data in milliseconds, calculating the probability that this was an attack. As the confidence grew, the system did something remarkable—it predicted what would happen next. Based on similar patterns from past breaches, it knew the intruder would likely attempt to escalate privileges and move laterally through the network.

Before Jonah could even reach for his keyboard, the AI took action. It created a digital sandbox around the suspicious activity, allowing the intruder to think they were still inside the real system while actually being isolated. The attacker tried to access more sensitive files, unaware that every move was being watched, recorded, and analyzed. To them, everything looked normal. To the defense system, it was a controlled experiment.

The intruder's AI-driven tools tried to adapt, changing tactics to avoid detection. But the defense AI adapted faster, learning from each move and closing off every escape route. It was like watching two invisible minds racing against each other in the dark. Jonah felt a surge of excitement as the system's confidence reached one hundred percent. The threat was real—and it was contained.

Within minutes, the attacker was locked out completely. Their access vanished, their tools rendered useless. The company's data remained untouched, its customers unaware of how close they had come to disaster. Jonah leaned back in his chair, heart still pounding. The breach had been stopped not after it happened, but before it truly began.

As the AI logged the incident and updated its models, Jonah

realized he had just witnessed the future of cybersecurity. No frantic phone calls. No emergency shutdowns. Just a quiet, intelligent system that saw the danger coming and eliminated it before anyone got hurt. In a world of invisible wars, this was the kind of guardian humanity desperately needed.

Chapter 3

Automated Response: How AI Stops Attacks Without Human Delay

In the modern cyber battlefield, detecting an attack is only half the fight. The true difference between security and catastrophe lies in how fast a system can respond. Cyberattacks today unfold at machine speed, often completing in seconds what once took days. Ransomware can encrypt entire networks in minutes. Data exfiltration can move terabytes of sensitive information across borders before a human analyst even sees an alert. This is why automated response, powered by artificial intelligence, has become the backbone of modern cyber defense. AI does not merely observe threats—it acts, making decisions and executing defensive actions in real time, without waiting for human approval.

Automated AI response systems operate through a concept known as orchestration. When a threat is detected, the AI evaluates the severity, scope, and potential impact of the attack. It then selects the appropriate countermeasures from a vast library of defensive actions. These may include isolating a compromised device, blocking suspicious IP addresses, revoking user credentials, shutting down malicious processes, or restoring files from secure backups. The system chooses the least disruptive response that will neutralize the threat, ensuring business operations continue while the danger is removed. This precision is what makes AI-driven automation both powerful and safe.

One of the greatest strengths of AI response systems is their ability to operate under uncertainty. In the early stages of an attack, not all information is available. A human might hesitate, unsure whether an anomaly is a glitch or a real threat. AI, however, works with probabilities. It can calculate the likelihood that an event is malicious based on thousands of variables and take action when that probability crosses a certain threshold. This allows it to intervene early, when damage is still minimal, rather than waiting for absolute certainty while the attack spreads.

AI-driven automation also enables organizations to scale their defenses. A single security team may be responsible for protecting thousands of systems across multiple locations and cloud environments. Without automation, this task is impossible. AI systems handle routine and high-speed responses, freeing human analysts to focus on investigation, strategy, and improvement. This human-AI partnership transforms cybersecurity from a reactive firefighting operation into a proactive, resilient defense. Another critical role of automated response is containment. Many cyberattacks rely on moving laterally through a network, jumping from one compromised system to another until they reach their target. AI can recognize this movement and instantly create digital barriers, isolating infected systems and cutting off communication between them. This prevents the attack from spreading, turning what could have been a massive breach into a small, manageable incident.

AI can also perform automated recovery. When ransomware encrypts files or malware modifies system settings, AI systems can reverse those changes by restoring data from secure backups or rolling systems back to a safe state. This dramatically reduces downtime and financial losses. Instead of waiting for IT teams to manually rebuild systems, organizations can return to normal operations almost immediately.

Trust is a major concern when it comes to automation. Giving machines the power to shut down systems, block users, or alter networks can be risky if not properly controlled. Modern AI cyber defense platforms address this by using layered decision-making, audit logs, and human oversight. Every automated action is recorded and can be reviewed, and high-risk decisions can be configured to require human confirmation. This balance ensures that organizations get the speed of automation without sacrificing control. Automated response also allows organizations to enforce security policies consistently. Humans make mistakes, overlook details, and become fatigued. AI applies rules and models the same way every time, ensuring that every threat is handled according to best practices. This consistency is essential in regulated industries such as finance, healthcare, and government, where even small security failures can have legal and ethical consequences.

As cyberattacks become more autonomous and aggressive, manual defense will simply not be enough. Attackers already use AI to launch thousands of simultaneous intrusions, probing every weakness they can find. The only way to counter this is with equally autonomous defense systems that can react just as quickly and intelligently. Automated AI response is not about replacing people—it is about giving them the tools they need to keep up with machine-speed threats.

The future of cybersecurity belongs to systems that can see, decide, and act in real time. AI-powered automated response closes the gap between detection and defense, ensuring that threats are neutralized the moment they appear. In a world where seconds matter, this capability is the difference between a near miss and a digital disaster.

"Sixty Seconds to Zero"

The countdown had already begun when Evelyn noticed the first spike in network traffic. It wasn't dramatic—just a quiet surge of encrypted data moving toward an unfamiliar server overseas. But the AI defense system had already connected the dots. In less than a second, it identified the pattern as an active data exfiltration attempt, the final stage of a sophisticated breach. If the transfer completed, millions of customer records would be lost.

Evelyn watched the dashboard as the AI took control. There was no frantic scrambling, no emergency phone calls. The system calculated the risk, selected its response, and acted. The compromised account was locked. The server was isolated. The data stream was cut off mid-transfer, leaving only fragments behind. To the attacker, it was as if the target had suddenly vanished.

The intruder's AI tried to fight back, launching new connections and shifting routes, but the defense AI was faster. It closed every door before it could be opened, sealing off the digital environment like a submarine under attack. Within sixty seconds, the breach was completely neutralized.

Evelyn exhaled, barely realizing she had been holding her breath. The company's data was safe. The customers would never know how close they had come to disaster. As the AI logged the incident and restored normal operations, Evelyn felt a quiet pride. This was what the future of security looked like—not chaos and panic, but calm, intelligent systems standing guard.

In a world where machines attacked at the speed of light, only machines could defend just as fast. And today, the defense had won.

Chapter 4

Behavioral Analysis and Predictive Threat Intelligence

Modern cyberattacks rarely begin with obvious explosions of malicious code. Instead, they unfold quietly, often hiding in plain sight while attackers carefully probe, observe, and adapt. This is why behavioral analysis has become one of the most powerful tools in AI-powered cyber defense. Rather than focusing solely on what a piece of software is, AI looks at what it does. Every action—every login, every file access, every network request—becomes part of a behavioral pattern. By learning what normal behavior looks like for every user, device, and system, AI can detect even the smallest deviations that signal the presence of an intruder.

Behavioral analysis allows AI systems to build digital fingerprints of legitimate activity. For example, an employee may normally log in from a specific region, use certain applications, and access particular types of data. When that same account suddenly begins downloading large volumes of files at midnight from a foreign country, the AI immediately recognizes that something is wrong. Even if the attacker has valid credentials, their behavior does not match the established profile. This ability to detect identity misuse is critical in a world where stolen passwords and deepfake-driven impersonation are increasingly common.

Predictive threat intelligence takes behavioral analysis a step further by allowing AI to anticipate attacks before they fully materialize. By studying historical attack patterns, global threat data, and real-time network activity, AI systems can forecast what an attacker is likely to do next. If a suspicious login is followed by reconnaissance activity, the AI can predict that lateral movement or data theft is coming and prepare defenses in advance. This turns cybersecurity into a game of anticipation rather than reaction, dramatically increasing the chances of stopping attacks early.

AI-powered predictive models continuously analyze trends across millions of systems worldwide. When a new type of attack emerges in one region, the knowledge is quickly shared across networks, allowing defenses elsewhere to be updated instantly. This global intelligence network means that an attack discovered in one organization can help protect thousands of others. In this way, AI transforms cybersecurity into a collective immune system, where every attempted breach strengthens the defenses of the entire digital ecosystem.

Behavioral analysis is also essential for detecting insider threats. Not all cyber risks come from external hackers. Employees, contractors, and partners can intentionally or accidentally cause harm. AI monitors internal behavior just as closely as external activity, identifying when someone begins acting in ways that could indicate data theft, sabotage, or negligence. By detecting these patterns early, organizations can intervene before serious damage occurs.

One of the most powerful aspects of behavioral AI is its ability to evolve alongside its environment. As businesses grow, adopt new tools, and change their workflows, the AI updates its understanding of normal behavior. This prevents security systems from becoming outdated or overly restrictive. Instead of forcing organizations to adapt to rigid rules, AI adapts to the organization, providing protection that fits its unique digital DNA.

Predictive threat intelligence also plays a crucial role in strategic cybersecurity planning. By analyzing long-term trends, AI can identify which systems are most likely to be targeted, which vulnerabilities are being exploited most frequently, and which attack methods are gaining popularity. This allows organizations to prioritize investments, strengthen weak points, and prepare for emerging threats before they become widespread. In an era of AI-powered attacks, behavior is the new signature. Hackers can disguise their code, encrypt their traffic, and spoof their identities, but they cannot hide their actions. AI-powered behavioral analysis shines a light on these hidden movements, revealing the true intent behind every digital interaction. Combined with predictive intelligence, it gives defenders the ability to see the future of an attack before it happens.

This shift from static defense to dynamic, predictive protection marks a turning point in cybersecurity. Instead of constantly reacting to crises, organizations can now stay ahead of their adversaries, stopping threats before they escalate. Behavioral AI does not just protect systems—it gives them foresight, turning cybersecurity into a proactive and strategic discipline rather than a desperate race against time.

"The Pattern No One Could See"

No one noticed the intruder at first—not the engineers, not the executives, not even the human security team. The attacker had the perfect disguise: valid credentials, normal login times, and access to all the right systems. To the untrained eye, everything looked routine. But the AI was watching, and it noticed something that no one else could see.

The account began accessing files in a slightly different order than usual. It paused for fractions of a second longer between actions. It touched data that the real user rarely needed. These were tiny details, invisible to humans but glaring to a system that understood behavior at a microscopic level. The AI quietly began to build a probability model. Something was wrong.

As the intruder moved deeper into the network, the AI predicted what would happen next. Based on thousands of past attacks, it knew that the next step would likely be data exfiltration. Before the attacker could even start the transfer, the defense system prepared a trap. It created a decoy environment filled with fake files and false pathways, guiding the intruder away from the real data.

The attacker took the bait. Believing they were stealing valuable information, they moved into the decoy system, unaware that they were now completely isolated. Every action was recorded, every technique analyzed. By the time they realized something was wrong, it was too late. Their access was cut off, their tools neutralized.

When the real user logged in later that day, they never knew their identity had been stolen. The data was safe. The network was secure. And somewhere deep inside the digital infrastructure, the AI quietly updated its models, ready for the next pattern that didn't belong.

In a world of perfect disguises, it was behavior that betrayed the enemy—and AI that saw what no human ever could.

Chapter 5

AI Defense for Cloud, Endpoints, and Zero-Trust Networks

As organizations move deeper into cloud computing, remote work, and mobile technology, the idea of a single, well-defined network perimeter has disappeared. Employees log in from home offices, airports, coffee shops, and mobile devices. Applications run across multiple cloud providers. Data flows constantly between internal systems and third-party services. This new digital reality has created an environment where trust can no longer be assumed based on location or device alone. In this landscape, AI-powered cyber defense becomes the central nervous system that connects, monitors, and protects every part of the organization in real time.

Cloud environments are especially complex. Servers are created and destroyed automatically, workloads shift between regions, and applications scale up and down in response to demand. Traditional security tools struggle to keep up with this constant motion. AI, however, is designed for dynamic environments. It continuously maps the cloud infrastructure, learning how services communicate, where data is stored, and how users interact with resources. When something deviates from the normal flow—such as a workload accessing sensitive data without authorization or a cloud instance suddenly sending information to an unknown destination—the AI flags and responds instantly.

Endpoints—laptops, phones, tablets, and IoT devices—are often the weakest link in cybersecurity. These devices are used by people in uncontrolled environments and are frequently targeted by phishing, malware, and credential theft. AI-powered endpoint protection goes far beyond traditional antivirus software. It monitors how each device behaves, which applications it runs, and how it interacts with the network. If a device starts acting suspiciously, the AI can isolate it from the rest of the system, preventing an infection from spreading while the issue is resolved.

Zero-trust security is a philosophy that assumes no user or device should ever be trusted by default. Every access request must be verified, every action continuously evaluated. AI makes zero-trust practical. It analyzes identity, behavior, location, device health, and risk in real time, granting or denying access based on a constantly updated risk score. A user who logs in from a known device in a normal location may be granted full access, while the same user logging in from a new country or an infected device may be restricted or blocked. This dynamic decision-making is impossible without AI. AI also plays a crucial role in securing application programming interfaces, or APIs, which connect modern digital systems. APIs are often targeted by attackers because they provide direct access to data and functionality. AI monitors API traffic, learning what normal usage looks like and detecting abnormal requests that could indicate abuse, scraping, or data theft. This protects not only internal systems but also customer-facing services such as mobile apps, financial platforms, and online marketplaces.

In a zero-trust, cloud-first world, identity is the new perimeter. AI continuously evaluates who a user is, how they behave, and what they are trying to do. This allows organizations to grant just-enough access while minimizing risk. If an account is compromised, the attacker's behavior will quickly diverge from the real user's pattern, triggering defensive actions. This prevents stolen credentials from becoming a gateway to full system compromise.

AI-driven defense also improves visibility across fragmented digital environments. Many organizations use multiple cloud providers, on-premise systems, and third-party platforms. AI unifies these into a single security view, correlating events and detecting threats that span multiple systems. This holistic awareness is essential for stopping modern attacks, which often move across different platforms to avoid detection. The combination of cloud, endpoint, and zero-trust security creates a layered defense that adapts to the way people actually work. Instead of forcing rigid rules on a fluid digital world, AI provides flexible, intelligent protection that follows users and data wherever they go. This ensures that security is not a barrier to productivity but an invisible shield that works quietly in the background.

As cyber threats grow more sophisticated, the environments they target grow more distributed. AI-powered cyber defense is the only technology capable of protecting this new digital frontier. By securing cloud platforms, endpoints, and identities in real time, AI ensures that no matter where work happens, protection is always present.

"No Safe Place"

Liam was working from a café in Lisbon when the attack began. To him, everything seemed normal: a strong Wi-Fi connection, his company laptop, and a steaming cup of coffee. But somewhere deep in the cloud, the AI defense system noticed something strange. His device had just made a request to an API it had never accessed before, asking for sensitive financial data. The risk score jumped instantly.

Within milliseconds, the AI evaluated Liam's identity, location, and behavior. The request didn't match his normal work patterns. Without alerting the attacker who had hijacked his session, the system quietly restricted access, allowing only low-risk actions to continue. The intruder tried again, escalating the request, but every path was blocked.

Meanwhile, the AI isolated Liam's laptop from the rest of the network, protecting other systems while still allowing him to keep working. Liam had no idea anything was wrong—until a message appeared asking him to re-authenticate. The attacker was gone.

Across continents and cloud platforms, the AI had done its job. There was no safe place for the attack to hide, no weak perimeter to slip through. In a world without borders, the defense was everywhere.

Chapter 6

Continuous Monitoring and AI Threat Hunting

In the ever-evolving landscape of cybersecurity, threats do not arrive on a predictable schedule. Cybercriminals operate 24/7, and attacks can emerge at any hour, from anywhere in the world. The sheer scale and speed of these attacks make human monitoring alone insufficient. AI-powered continuous monitoring provides a perpetual, vigilant presence across networks, endpoints, and cloud infrastructures. Unlike traditional tools that only act when a threshold is crossed, continuous monitoring allows AI to observe, analyze, and predict suspicious activity in real time, ensuring that no anomaly goes unnoticed. Every user action, system process, network transaction, and application behavior is recorded, analyzed, and contextualized, creating a dynamic map of the organization's digital environment. The AI does not merely log events; it interprets them, learning which behaviors are benign, which are unusual, and which are indicative of evolving threats. By correlating millions of data points from diverse sources, AI can detect patterns that would be invisible to human analysts, such as subtle reconnaissance activity or low-and-slow malware behavior that gradually escalates over weeks. This level of insight transforms cybersecurity from reactive to proactive, enabling organizations to respond to threats before they materialize into full-scale breaches.

Continuous monitoring is especially crucial for detecting advanced persistent threats (APTs), which are carefully orchestrated attacks designed to infiltrate a system and remain undetected for extended periods. These attacks often involve multiple stages: initial compromise, lateral movement, privilege escalation, and eventual exfiltration of sensitive data. Human teams may only notice the attack after damage has already been done, but AI monitoring identifies anomalies at each stage. Even slight deviations from normal login patterns, data access sequences, or command executions can be flagged, allowing the AI to intercede in milliseconds. The system can automatically isolate compromised devices, revoke suspicious sessions, and alert security teams with prioritized information, ensuring that humans focus on meaningful threats rather than sifting through thousands of false positives.

AI threat hunting builds upon continuous monitoring by actively searching for hidden dangers rather than waiting for them to trigger alerts. Traditional security relies on known indicators of compromise, such as virus signatures or blacklisted IP addresses. In contrast, AI threat hunting uses predictive models, behavioral analysis, and anomaly detection to uncover potential threats before they execute. The system can simulate attack scenarios, evaluate the risk of unusual behavior, and prioritize potential threats based on their likelihood and potential impact. By constantly probing the network, endpoints, and cloud services, AI identifies vulnerabilities, latent malware, or suspicious user activity that might otherwise go unnoticed. This preemptive approach is critical in environments where attackers use highly sophisticated tools, such as AI-driven malware that adapts in real time, polymorphic ransomware that changes its signature, and social engineering attacks that exploit human psychology to gain access.

An essential aspect of continuous monitoring and threat hunting is contextual awareness. AI does not treat all anomalies equally; it evaluates them in the context of the organization's environment. For instance, a user logging in from a different city might be routine if they are traveling for business but suspicious if the login occurs at an unusual hour or from a device the AI has never seen. Similarly, a server sending large volumes of data may be normal during a scheduled backup but abnormal if the timing, destination, or volume is irregular. By incorporating contextual intelligence, AI reduces false positives, focuses attention on genuine threats, and enhances the precision of automated responses. This makes AI not just a monitor but a strategic assistant, guiding security teams toward the most critical issues and enabling them to make informed decisions quickly.

Continuous monitoring also extends to external threat intelligence. AI systems gather data from global sources, including known attack campaigns, malware signatures, threat actor behavior, and zero-day exploit trends. By integrating this information into its internal monitoring, AI can anticipate attacks targeting specific industries, technologies, or geographies. When a new threat emerges anywhere in the world, the AI can adjust its models to detect similar activity within the organization, effectively creating a collective defense network. This global awareness ensures that organizations are not only protected against known threats but also prepared for emerging and previously unseen attack vectors.

Another advantage of continuous AI monitoring is its ability to track supply chain and third-party risks. Modern organizations depend on an ecosystem of vendors, partners, and cloud services, any of which can introduce vulnerabilities. AI monitors interactions between these entities, identifies anomalies, and assesses the risk posed by external connections. If a third-party system is compromised, AI can prevent the infection from spreading into the organization's network. By continuously evaluating these external dependencies, AI enables organizations to maintain security across an extended, interconnected environment.

AI's role in continuous monitoring also encompasses compliance and audit readiness. Many industries require organizations to maintain detailed logs, enforce access policies, and demonstrate that security controls are effective. AI can automatically record all events, track actions taken, and provide reports in real time, simplifying regulatory compliance. This not only reduces operational overhead but also ensures that organizations can respond to audits, investigations, or legal inquiries with accurate and verifiable data. By integrating monitoring, threat hunting, and compliance functions, AI creates a unified cybersecurity ecosystem that is resilient, efficient, and adaptive.

Ultimately, continuous monitoring and AI threat hunting shift the paradigm from passive defense to active protection. Organizations no longer have to wait for attacks to reveal themselves or rely on human vigilance alone. Instead, AI operates as a constant guardian, detecting, analyzing, and responding to threats in real time while simultaneously preparing the organization for future risks. This proactive, intelligent approach ensures that even the most sophisticated cybercriminals face a formidable adversary, one that never sleeps, never forgets, and continuously improves. The future of cybersecurity lies in this dynamic, always-on defense model, where AI is not just a tool but an indispensable partner in protecting critical digital assets.

"The Night the Network Never Slept"

It was two o'clock in the morning when the first anomaly appeared, a barely perceptible ripple across the global financial network. To a human observer, nothing seemed out of the ordinary. The servers hummed, user accounts logged in and out as expected, and data flowed smoothly between branches in New York, London, and Singapore. But the AI that monitored the system never slept. It noticed the microsecond discrepancies, the unusual sequence of API calls, the subtle deviations from established patterns. Something—or someone—was probing the network, moving carefully, like a shadow navigating a maze.

Within moments, the AI began mapping the intruder's movements, correlating them across devices, servers, and user accounts. It recognized the signature of an advanced persistent threat: a team of hackers using AI-driven malware that could adapt in real time, evade detection, and slowly escalate privileges. They were trying to access accounts one by one, looking for a way into the treasure trove of sensitive financial data. What they didn't realize was that the network they had chosen to attack was alive in a way no human had ever seen before.

The AI launched its own countermeasures, quietly and invisibly. It began isolating compromised nodes, creating decoys, and feeding false information to the intruder's malware. Each action was calculated, based on predictive models that anticipated what the attackers would do next. When the hackers attempted lateral movement, the AI redirected them into virtual corridors lined with traps, simulating the real environment while keeping the actual data safe. Every step they took was recorded, every technique analyzed, and every pattern learned to improve future defenses.

Meanwhile, human analysts like Aisha, stationed in the security operations center, observed the incident unfold through a dashboard filled with alerts, probabilities, and real-time visualizations. To her, it looked almost like a game of chess being played at impossible speed. But she understood the stakes: this was not a simulation. Millions of financial records, corporate secrets, and customer accounts were at risk. Yet the AI operated with calm precision, handling what would have required hundreds of people working around the clock.

Hours passed, and the attack escalated. The intruders tried to manipulate network traffic, bypass controls, and introduce polymorphic malware designed to evade detection. Every tactic, every new angle, was anticipated by the AI. It adapted instantaneously, deploying new decoys, blocking malicious connections, and adjusting monitoring rules across the entire global infrastructure. At no point did the attackers realize they were trapped in a carefully controlled environment.

By dawn, the intruders had given up, unable to breach the defenses. Their tools had been neutralized, their plans meticulously recorded for forensic analysis, and their access completely severed. The AI updated its predictive models, ensuring that the next attempt, no matter how sophisticated, would face an even stronger barrier. The network had not just survived—it had fought back, learned from the encounter, and emerged more resilient than ever.

Aisha leaned back in her chair, exhausted but exhilarated. She thought about how different this was from the old days of cybersecurity: frantic alerts, panicked phone calls, and endless nights trying to patch holes after damage had already been done. Now, with AI continuously monitoring, hunting, and responding, the network itself was an active defender. It never slept, it never tired, and it had just proven that even the most advanced threats could be contained without a single human intervention in the critical moments. The digital battlefield had changed forever, and for the first time, the defenders were ahead.

Chapter 7

AI Incident Response and Post-Attack Forensics

Even the most sophisticated AI-powered defenses cannot prevent every single attack. Despite predictive threat models, continuous monitoring, and automated interventions, determined attackers may occasionally breach a system. When this occurs, the speed and precision of incident response become critical. AI incident response systems are designed to manage these crises efficiently, minimizing damage, maintaining business continuity, and enabling rapid recovery. Unlike traditional approaches that require human teams to manually investigate, contain, and remediate an incident, AI can automatically orchestrate the steps required to respond to breaches in real time, ensuring that every action is accurate, coordinated, and optimized for speed. From isolating compromised nodes to rolling back affected systems, AI ensures that incidents are addressed with machine-level precision, leaving humans free to focus on strategy, analysis, and decision-making.

One of the key elements of AI incident response is automated containment. When an attack is detected, the system can instantly quarantine infected devices, block malicious IP addresses, disable compromised accounts, and prevent the spread of malware. This immediate action is essential in limiting the scope of a breach. In conventional security models, these decisions often require approval from human analysts, introducing delays that attackers exploit. AI removes this latency by assessing risk and taking calculated action without waiting for confirmation, dramatically reducing the potential impact of an attack. Simultaneously, the system logs every action, creating a comprehensive record that can be reviewed, audited, and refined over time.

After containment, the focus shifts to remediation and recovery. AI incident response platforms can automatically restore files from secure backups, reverse malicious configuration changes, and repair affected systems to their pre-incident state. Unlike manual recovery processes, which are prone to error and require significant time, AI systems execute these tasks with consistency and precision. The result is reduced downtime, minimized financial loss, and continuity of operations. In industries like finance, healthcare, and critical infrastructure, where even short outages can have catastrophic consequences, this capability is invaluable. AI ensures that organizations can recover from incidents almost as quickly as they occur, maintaining operational resilience in the face of sophisticated attacks. An essential component of post-attack analysis is AI-driven forensics. Understanding how an attacker gained access, which systems were targeted, and what vulnerabilities were exploited is critical for improving defenses. AI can process enormous volumes of log data, system events, network traffic, and user activity to reconstruct the entire attack sequence. Unlike traditional forensic teams that manually review logs, AI identifies patterns, correlates events across multiple systems, and highlights anomalies that indicate the attacker's techniques. This allows organizations to learn from each incident, update their defenses, and prevent similar attacks in the future. Over time, AI becomes smarter, continuously refining its detection models based on real-world experience.

AI also assists in attributing attacks to specific actors or techniques. By analyzing indicators such as malware signatures, command-and-control patterns, phishing tactics, and even behavioral traits of the attacker, AI can provide insight into the origins and methods of a breach. This information is critical for legal, regulatory, and strategic purposes. Organizations can report attacks with precise evidence, strengthen compliance with cybersecurity regulations, and collaborate with law enforcement when necessary. Furthermore, this attribution helps the AI system anticipate future threats, allowing proactive defense against similar attack strategies. Another advantage of AI incident response is scalability. Modern enterprises often operate across multiple cloud environments, thousands of endpoints, and globally distributed networks. Coordinating a human-led response in such an environment is nearly impossible. AI can simultaneously manage containment, remediation, and forensics across every system in real time. Every node, server, and device becomes part of an integrated defense and recovery operation, ensuring that no element of the network is overlooked. This level of orchestration is beyond the capacity of human teams alone, making AI indispensable in complex digital environments.

AI incident response systems are also adaptive. Each attack, whether successful or blocked, provides new data that the AI uses to refine its models. Threat intelligence gathered from post-attack analysis informs future detection, containment strategies, and response protocols. This creates a continuously improving security ecosystem where every incident strengthens defenses, turning failures into learning opportunities. Over time, the system becomes increasingly effective at preventing breaches, detecting subtle signs of compromise, and responding to attacks before they escalate.

Finally, AI enables organizations to integrate incident response with broader cybersecurity strategies. Automated playbooks, risk scoring, and predictive threat intelligence allow for coordinated defense across detection, monitoring, response, and recovery. AI systems can even simulate potential attack scenarios, testing defenses and identifying weaknesses proactively. This combination of reactive and proactive capabilities ensures that organizations are not merely surviving attacks—they are learning, evolving, and growing stronger with every encounter.

The rise of AI incident response and post-attack forensics has transformed the way organizations approach cybersecurity. No longer is protection a static, reactive process. It is dynamic, intelligent, and continuously improving. Even when attacks occur, AI ensures that they are contained, analyzed, and leveraged to strengthen future defenses. In an era of relentless, automated, and AI-driven threats, incident response powered by artificial intelligence is the cornerstone of resilience, enabling organizations to survive and thrive in the most hostile digital environments.

"The Breach That Taught the Network"

It began subtly, almost imperceptibly. At first, Maya's dashboard showed nothing unusual. Network traffic appeared normal, users logged in as expected, and systems hummed along without disruption. But the AI noticed tiny irregularities: a series of login attempts from a remote server, a user account accessing files outside of its normal workflow, and encrypted packets moving to an unknown endpoint. Individually, each event seemed minor. Together, they formed a pattern that the AI recognized as the early stages of a sophisticated intrusion.

Within milliseconds, the AI took action. The affected devices were isolated, suspicious connections blocked, and a virtual containment zone was established. The intruder believed they were moving freely, exploring the network, testing defenses. Meanwhile, the AI quietly analyzed every action, reconstructing the sequence of the attack as it unfolded. Maya, watching from the security operations center, could barely follow the speed of the system. Actions were happening faster than any human could process, yet the network remained entirely under control.

The attacker tried lateral movement, hopping from server to server, escalating privileges, and attempting to access sensitive financial databases. Each move was anticipated. The AI predicted the likely path of the intrusion and reinforced defenses along the route, guiding the intruder into decoy environments filled with simulated data. Every file accessed was a trap. Every command executed was observed and recorded. The attackers, confident in their strategy, had no idea that the network itself was learning, adapting, and fighting back.

As the night wore on, the AI began executing automated remediation protocols. Systems that had been altered were rolled back to their last safe state. Malware traces were eliminated. Access permissions were restored to their proper configuration. By the time the human team arrived to review the incident, the AI had already neutralized the threat. No critical data had been stolen, no systems had been permanently damaged, and the network had recorded every detail of the intrusion for post-attack analysis.

Post-attack forensics revealed not only how the breach occurred but also the methods and tactics of the intruders. The AI analyzed every step, identifying vulnerabilities that had been exploited and recommending changes to prevent similar attempts in the future. Each lesson learned fed back into the system, strengthening predictive models and detection protocols. By dawn, the AI had not only stopped the attack but had also improved the network's defenses for the next one.

Maya marveled at how the AI had transformed incident response. In a previous era, this breach could have caused weeks of disruption, millions of dollars in losses, and permanent reputational damage. Now, it was a controlled learning experience. The network had adapted, evolved, and emerged stronger, turning an attempted disaster into a strategic advantage. The AI had taught the organization a crucial lesson: in the era of intelligent threats, survival depends not just on defense, but on the ability to learn faster than the attacker.

By the end of the day, the intruders had given up. Their tools were neutralized, their access revoked, and their actions meticulously recorded for investigation. The network had anticipated, contained, and recovered from the attack without human intervention during the critical moments. Maya realized the profound shift in cybersecurity: protection was no longer reactive. It was intelligent, continuous, and adaptive. The network had learned, and with AI as its guardian, it would never forget.

In that quiet moment, Maya understood the future of cybersecurity: every breach, every intrusion, and every attempt to compromise the system would serve as a lesson, making the AI smarter, the network stronger, and the organization virtually unbreakable. In the digital age, survival would belong to those who could learn faster than their adversaries—and tonight, the network had proven it could.

Chapter 8

Adaptive AI and the Future of Autonomous Cyber Defense

Cybersecurity in the modern era is no longer a static discipline. Threats evolve constantly, using artificial intelligence themselves to probe, bypass, and exploit vulnerabilities. Attackers leverage machine learning, autonomous malware, and polymorphic ransomware that adapts in real time, creating a landscape in which traditional defense tools are increasingly ineffective. This environment has given rise to adaptive AI in cybersecurity—systems capable not only of detecting and responding to attacks but also of learning, evolving, and improving continuously based on every interaction. Adaptive AI shifts cybersecurity from a reactive process into a self-improving, autonomous defense ecosystem that can anticipate threats, refine countermeasures, and optimize protective strategies without human intervention. The intelligence of the system grows in real time, using data from ongoing operations, past breaches, and global threat intelligence networks, creating a digital defense infrastructure that is resilient, agile, and perpetually learning.

At the heart of adaptive AI is machine learning, which enables the system to identify patterns, correlations, and anomalies across immense datasets. The AI constantly ingests log data, network traffic, endpoint activity, cloud events, and user behavior. It evaluates millions of events per second, discerning which behaviors are normal, which are potentially risky, and which constitute malicious activity. The system then adjusts its models based on this continuous input, improving its accuracy in detecting both known and unknown threats. Unlike traditional rule-based systems, which can become outdated as attackers innovate, adaptive AI evolves alongside the threat landscape, ensuring defenses remain relevant and robust against emerging attack vectors. This evolution allows organizations to defend against attacks that are unprecedented, unpredictable, or specifically targeted at them.

One of the most powerful aspects of adaptive AI is its ability to integrate predictive threat intelligence. By analyzing historical attack data, threat feeds, and global cybersecurity events, AI can anticipate the methods and targets of future attacks. For example, if a ransomware strain has begun spreading through a specific type of cloud service, the AI can proactively scan, isolate, and protect vulnerable assets across the organization before the malware even arrives. This foresight transforms cybersecurity from a game of reaction to one of anticipation, giving organizations the ability to stay ahead of sophisticated attackers who rely on speed, automation, and deception. Predictive intelligence also allows AI to suggest proactive security measures, such as patching specific vulnerabilities, enforcing stricter access controls, or segmenting network environments, minimizing exposure before a breach can occur.

Adaptive AI excels in environments where human oversight alone is insufficient. Large organizations often operate across thousands of endpoints, multiple cloud providers, and globally distributed networks. Manual monitoring and response are impractical, and even highly skilled human teams cannot process the volume and speed of events occurring every second. Adaptive AI provides continuous surveillance, correlating activity across disparate systems, identifying subtle attack indicators, and executing defensive actions instantaneously. This real-time capability ensures that threats are neutralized before they escalate, and that attackers are forced to navigate a digital ecosystem that adapts faster than they can respond.

Another critical component of adaptive AI is its ability to orchestrate automated defense responses. When a threat is detected, the AI does not merely alert human operators; it takes immediate action. Compromised devices can be isolated, malicious processes terminated, data transfers blocked, and suspicious accounts disabled automatically. The AI continuously evaluates the effectiveness of these interventions, adjusting tactics as attackers attempt to circumvent defenses.

This feedback loop ensures that the system is not static but dynamically responds to changes in the attack landscape. Over time, the AI becomes more efficient, learning which interventions are most effective under different circumstances, and refining its playbooks to minimize damage and downtime.

Adaptive AI also enhances the protection of cloud environments, endpoints, and zero-trust networks. Cloud platforms are highly dynamic, with workloads shifting between regions, users accessing systems remotely, and applications scaling automatically. Adaptive AI continuously maps these environments, understanding normal behavior and detecting deviations that indicate potential breaches. Endpoints, including laptops, mobile devices, and IoT systems, are similarly monitored in real time. The AI identifies behavioral anomalies, isolates compromised devices, and prevents lateral movement of attackers, ensuring that threats cannot spread unchecked. In zero-trust architectures, adaptive AI constantly evaluates risk scores for users, devices, and applications, granting access only when behavior and context align with trusted patterns.

The integration of post-incident learning is another feature of adaptive AI that sets it apart from traditional security models. Every detected attack, whether fully blocked or partially successful, is analyzed for lessons. Attack vectors, tactics, techniques, and procedures are incorporated into the AI's models, strengthening predictive capabilities and future responses. This creates a cycle in which the system becomes smarter with every attempt, transforming the network into a self-improving, self-defending organism. Unlike human teams, which may forget or misinterpret details, adaptive AI preserves institutional knowledge indefinitely, ensuring that every attack contributes to long-term resilience.

Adaptive AI is also designed to collaborate seamlessly with human teams. While it can operate autonomously, human operators remain essential for strategy, high-risk decision-making, and oversight. AI provides prioritized alerts, contextual analysis, and recommended actions, allowing security teams to focus on critical tasks rather than chasing false positives or performing repetitive investigations. This human-AI partnership magnifies the capabilities of both, creating a hybrid defense ecosystem that combines speed, accuracy, and strategic insight.

Finally, adaptive AI represents the future of autonomous cybersecurity. It is the only technology capable of continuously evolving to match the pace of modern cyber threats. By combining continuous monitoring, predictive intelligence, automated response, behavioral analysis, and post-incident learning, adaptive AI creates a digital defense system that is proactive, intelligent, and resilient. Organizations that implement these systems gain a decisive advantage over attackers, achieving not just protection, but strategic foresight, operational continuity, and long-term security. In an era where AI-driven attacks can emerge at any moment, adaptive AI ensures that networks are not only defended but prepared, capable of learning, evolving, and thriving against an intelligent adversary.

"The Day the AI Learned to Fight Alone"

It was just before midnight when the first signs of intrusion appeared. Unlike previous attacks, which were chaotic and noisy, this one was deliberate, silent, and almost invisible. Across the company's global network, a hacker AI had been probing endpoints, testing access credentials, and moving laterally with surgical precision. Human operators were asleep, their dashboards quiet except for routine system activity. But the adaptive AI never rested. It detected the subtle irregularities in device behavior, small timing discrepancies, and unusual sequences of access requests that indicated someone was inside the perimeter. It immediately began tracking the intruder, building a real-time model of the attack as it unfolded.

The AI first isolated the initial points of compromise, quietly redirecting the attacker into decoy systems that appeared real but contained no valuable data. Each time the intruder tried to pivot, escalate privileges, or exfiltrate files, the AI adapted, anticipating moves and closing paths. The attacker's own AI tools attempted to adjust, trying to mask their activity with complex patterns, but the defense AI learned faster. It predicted the intruder's next steps before they happened, deploying traps, sandboxing malware, and neutralizing malicious processes with precision. Every action was recorded, every attempt analyzed, and the results fed directly into the AI's models.

Hours passed in a tense digital cat-and-mouse game. The intruder tried multiple tactics: encrypted traffic meant to conceal exfiltration, fake API requests to confuse monitoring systems, and simulated user behavior to blend in with normal patterns. The adaptive AI responded dynamically, adjusting its detection thresholds, recalibrating its risk scores, and reinforcing vulnerable systems in real time. Devices that were exposed were automatically isolated, critical data was mirrored into protected containers, and lateral movement was cut off before it could reach sensitive assets. The network had become a self-defending organism, aware of every movement and capable of instantaneous intervention.

Maya, overseeing the operations center remotely, watched the system's response unfold on her monitor. Lines of code and activity streams flashed across the dashboard, representing actions the AI took in milliseconds. She realized with awe that the AI was operating autonomously, without human input, yet with flawless coordination. The intruder had no idea they were being studied, trapped, and redirected at every step. It was as if the network itself had grown consciousness, learning from each intrusion attempt and becoming smarter with every maneuver.

By dawn, the breach had been fully neutralized. The attacker's AI tools were isolated, their attempts logged, and their access revoked. The network had not just defended itself; it had analyzed, learned, and evolved. Every piece of malware, every suspicious login, every lateral movement had contributed to the system's growing intelligence. Predictive models were updated, new response protocols automatically integrated, and future defenses fortified. Human operators arriving at their workstations only saw the aftermath: normal operations continuing, data secure, and an AI that had fought alone and won.

Maya leaned back in her chair, reflecting on what she had witnessed. In the past, security teams had reacted to breaches with panic and exhaustion, often days behind attackers. Now, with adaptive AI, the network had anticipated, contained, and neutralized the attack entirely on its own. It had learned in real time, improved its own defenses, and ensured that a similar attempt in the future would face an even more formidable obstacle. The digital battlefield had changed forever. The AI had not just defended—it had become a teacher, a strategist, and a guardian, capable of outthinking the adversary before they even knew they were engaged.

In that quiet morning moment, Maya realized the profound truth: in the era of autonomous cyber threats, networks would survive not because of human vigilance alone, but because adaptive AI had learned to fight—and to win—without ever sleeping.

Chapter 9

AI-Driven Cybersecurity Analytics and Compliance

In today's digital world, organizations are required not only to protect their networks but also to demonstrate compliance with an ever-growing array of regulations, standards, and policies. From GDPR and CCPA to industry-specific frameworks like HIPAA, PCI-DSS, and NIST, the legal and regulatory landscape is complex and constantly evolving. Failure to comply can result in heavy fines, reputational damage, and even operational shutdowns. AI-driven cybersecurity analytics addresses this challenge by continuously monitoring systems, correlating events, and generating actionable insights that ensure both security and compliance. These systems analyze vast volumes of logs, endpoint data, network traffic, and user behavior to detect risks, uncover anomalies, and provide organizations with a clear, actionable view of their cybersecurity posture. Unlike human teams that must manually sift through thousands of reports, AI can process and interpret millions of data points in real time, identifying gaps, highlighting vulnerabilities, and producing compliance-ready evidence.

One of the most powerful aspects of AI in cybersecurity analytics is its ability to unify disparate data sources. Modern organizations operate across multiple cloud platforms, on-premise servers, mobile devices, and third-party services. Each of these generates its own logs and metrics, often in incompatible formats. AI systems normalize this data, integrate it into a single analytical model, and create correlations that humans would struggle to detect. For example, a failed login attempt on an endpoint might seem innocuous on its own, but when combined with unusual API calls in the cloud and a spike in outbound network traffic, AI can identify a coordinated breach attempt. This unified perspective allows organizations to see threats in context, prioritize response efforts, and document evidence for regulatory review.

Predictive analytics is another critical application of AI for compliance and security. By analyzing historical incidents, threat intelligence feeds, and behavioral patterns, AI can anticipate potential risks and suggest proactive measures. For instance, it can predict which systems are likely to be targeted next based on attack trends, which accounts might be vulnerable due to credential reuse or unusual behavior, and which processes could expose sensitive data. Organizations can then implement preemptive security measures, such as stricter access controls, enhanced monitoring, or patching critical vulnerabilities, reducing the likelihood of both breaches and regulatory violations. In this way, predictive AI shifts cybersecurity from reactive defense to proactive risk management.

AI also facilitates automated reporting and audit readiness. Traditional compliance audits are time-consuming, requiring IT teams to compile logs, track policy enforcement, and produce evidence of control effectiveness. AI systems continuously record, analyze, and summarize all security events, automatically generating reports that align with regulatory frameworks. These reports provide transparency, demonstrate adherence to required standards, and can be used to satisfy auditors, regulators, and stakeholders. The ability to produce accurate, real-time compliance documentation is particularly valuable in industries such as finance, healthcare, and critical infrastructure, where regulatory scrutiny is intense.

Behavioral analytics is a further advantage of AI-driven compliance. By continuously monitoring user and system activity, AI can identify deviations from established policies, highlight risky behavior, and trigger corrective action. This includes detecting unauthorized access attempts, abnormal data transfers, policy violations, and insider threats. Organizations can then enforce policies automatically or alert human operators for investigation, ensuring that security and compliance standards are maintained consistently. This continuous oversight reduces human error, strengthens governance, and enhances the organization's overall risk posture.

AI also assists in regulatory intelligence. Laws and frameworks are constantly evolving, with new rules and guidance issued regularly. Adaptive AI systems can ingest regulatory updates, interpret them in the context of the organization's operations, and adjust monitoring and controls accordingly. This ensures that cybersecurity and compliance measures remain up to date, reducing exposure to penalties and maintaining operational integrity. By integrating legal intelligence into real-time monitoring, AI creates a proactive compliance ecosystem where security controls and regulatory adherence are synchronized.

Furthermore, AI-driven analytics can support incident investigations and digital forensics. When a breach occurs, AI can reconstruct events across multiple systems, identifying root causes, mapping attack paths, and quantifying potential impact. This enables organizations to understand the full scope of incidents, improve defenses, and satisfy regulatory requirements for breach reporting. The ability to analyze complex attacks rapidly and accurately is critical, particularly when dealing with advanced persistent threats, multi-stage ransomware, or sophisticated social engineering campaigns. With AI, organizations can respond to incidents efficiently, comply with legal obligations, and prevent similar events in the future.

Ultimately, AI-driven cybersecurity analytics integrates security, risk management, and compliance into a unified, intelligent framework. By continuously monitoring activity, predicting threats, analyzing behavior, and supporting regulatory adherence, adaptive AI empowers organizations to defend against modern cyber threats while meeting legal and operational requirements. This combination of protection, insight, and accountability transforms cybersecurity from a reactive necessity into a strategic advantage, enabling organizations to operate safely, efficiently, and confidently in an increasingly complex digital environment. AI does not just secure systems—it ensures that organizations can demonstrate trust, transparency, and compliance in every digital interaction, providing a foundation for resilience and long-term success.

"The Audit That Never Felt Like One"

It was the first Monday of the quarter when the audit team arrived, laptops in hand, ready to scrutinize the company's cybersecurity practices. To most employees, this was a day of tension, a routine yet nerve-wracking exercise in proving compliance with GDPR, HIPAA, and internal security policies. But to Jordan Hayes, who oversaw the AI-driven security operations, it was almost anticlimactic. The AI system had already prepared for this moment months in advance, continuously monitoring activity, enforcing policies, and logging events in a detailed, organized manner. What had once taken days or weeks of manual reporting could now be demonstrated with a few clicks, and every piece of evidence was timestamped, contextualized, and verified in real time.

As the auditors began requesting logs, incident reports, and policy enforcement evidence, Jordan watched as the AI system generated comprehensive dashboards. Failed logins, privileged access requests, file transfer histories, endpoint behavior anomalies—all were neatly presented in digestible formats. Alerts were prioritized based on severity, correlated across systems, and cross-referenced against regulatory requirements. The auditors were impressed at the level of detail, but even more so at the speed. The AI provided not only historical evidence but also predictive insights, showing which accounts or systems were at risk and what measures had already been taken to mitigate potential issues. Jordan felt a quiet satisfaction knowing that this AI didn't just enforce rules; it actively improved security posture while creating a clear audit trail.

Midway through the review, a new alert appeared—a subtle anomaly in the cloud environment. A third-party application had requested access to sensitive files, but the AI immediately detected an irregular pattern. It isolated the connection, triggered a risk assessment, and created a detailed report showing why the access attempt was blocked. The auditors noticed and asked Jordan about the incident. “It’s routine,” Jordan explained. “The AI not only prevents unauthorized access but documents every action for compliance purposes. What would have taken hours to investigate manually is handled automatically in seconds.” The auditors nodded, clearly impressed at how seamlessly security, risk management, and compliance had been integrated.

As the day progressed, the AI continued to work autonomously, performing checks across endpoints, analyzing behavior, and generating actionable recommendations. It flagged minor policy deviations, provided remediation steps, and even simulated potential attack scenarios to ensure the organization was prepared for emerging threats. At no point did the auditors have to chase logs or question inconsistencies; the system anticipated every request. Jordan realized that AI had transformed what used to be a stressful, adversarial process into a smooth, proactive workflow. The audit became less about finding gaps and more about reviewing a continuously improving security ecosystem.

By late afternoon, the auditors had completed their review. They congratulated Jordan on the company's robust cybersecurity posture and the clarity of reporting. Jordan leaned back, reflecting on how different this process had become. In the past, audits were tedious, stressful, and often revealed shortcomings after the fact. Now, with adaptive AI monitoring, predictive analytics, and automated compliance reporting, the company had not only passed the audit but had strengthened its defenses while doing so. Every anomaly, every threat, and every security decision had been logged, analyzed, and incorporated into the system's models, ensuring that future audits would be even smoother.

As the auditors left, Jordan watched the AI continue its work, scanning endpoints, analyzing cloud traffic, and reinforcing policies. The network was never idle; it was constantly learning, adapting, and protecting. The day had proven that AI was more than a tool—it was a guardian, a strategist, and a compliance partner, ensuring security and regulatory adherence simultaneously. In the quiet hum of the operations center, Jordan realized the profound truth: in an era of relentless digital threats and complex regulations, survival and compliance would no longer depend on human effort alone. Adaptive AI had become the ultimate defender, continuously watching, learning, and evolving, turning every audit and every incident into an opportunity to strengthen the organization and outpace even the most sophisticated cyber adversaries. By nightfall, Jordan left the office knowing the network was prepared, not just for today's threats, but for the unknown attacks that would come tomorrow. The AI had observed, adapted, and ensured compliance seamlessly. In a world where regulatory scrutiny and cyberattacks were constant, the system had learned to operate autonomously, keeping the organization safe and accountable, and transforming what was once a burden into a competitive advantage. The AI had taught the humans that security and compliance were not separate functions but intertwined responsibilities, and that the network itself could now enforce, protect, and improve continuously.

Chapter 10

The Future of AI-Powered Cyber Defense: Autonomous Security and Global Resilience

As we reach the culmination of the AI-powered cybersecurity journey, it becomes clear that the future will be defined not by static firewalls or reactive defenses, but by autonomous, intelligent systems capable of thinking, adapting, and learning in real time. The convergence of artificial intelligence, machine learning, behavioral analysis, and predictive threat intelligence has already transformed the way organizations defend themselves. However, the evolution is only beginning. The next generation of AI cybersecurity will integrate autonomous response, self-healing networks, global threat intelligence sharing, and real-time predictive modeling to create digital ecosystems that are resilient, proactive, and virtually self-sufficient. In this vision, networks will not merely react to threats—they will anticipate them, neutralize them autonomously, and learn continuously from every interaction, whether human or machine-initiated.

Autonomous security will redefine the role of human cybersecurity teams. Rather than responding to alerts, investigating incidents, or manually enforcing policies, human professionals will focus on strategic planning, governance, and ethical oversight. AI systems will monitor every endpoint, network node, and cloud environment continuously, identifying anomalies, initiating containment, and executing remediation without waiting for human input. Advanced decision-making models will allow AI to weigh risk dynamically, selecting the most appropriate response based on context, potential impact, and predictive analytics. For example, a device behaving suspiciously in a low-risk segment may be monitored, while the same behavior in a critical system triggers immediate isolation and investigation. This contextual decision-making ensures optimal protection while minimizing operational disruption.

One of the defining features of future AI defense is self-healing infrastructure. Networks will be capable of automatically identifying vulnerabilities, patching systems, restoring compromised data, and reconfiguring resources without downtime. If an endpoint is infected with polymorphic malware, AI can isolate the device, remediate the infection, restore its integrity from secure backups, and return it to operation—all in a fraction of the time it would take a human team. This self-healing capability will dramatically reduce the operational and financial impact of cyberattacks, allowing organizations to maintain continuity in the face of increasingly sophisticated threats.

Global threat intelligence sharing will be another cornerstone of AI-powered defense. Organizations across industries and geographies will contribute anonymized attack data, enabling predictive AI models to recognize emerging threats even before they reach a given enterprise. If a ransomware campaign begins targeting a specific sector in Europe, organizations in North America will be protected proactively by AI models that have already learned the attack's signature, behavior patterns, and delivery methods. This creates a collective digital immune system, where each organization's defense strengthens the broader network of global cybersecurity.

AI will also integrate advanced predictive modeling to anticipate attacks in real time. By analyzing historical data, global trends, and behavioral anomalies, AI will forecast potential threats and recommend proactive actions. Systems will prioritize patching of critical vulnerabilities, adjust access controls dynamically, and even simulate attack scenarios to test resilience. Predictive AI will make cybersecurity a proactive discipline, where defenses are deployed before attacks occur, rather than relying solely on reactive measures.

Human-AI collaboration will remain critical, even as autonomous systems take a more central role. AI will provide context, recommendations, and actionable insights, while human experts focus on strategy, governance, and ethical considerations. Questions of privacy, regulatory compliance, and ethical deployment of AI in defense scenarios will require human oversight to ensure that autonomous systems operate within legal and moral boundaries. This symbiotic relationship between AI and humans will be essential for balancing operational efficiency with accountability, particularly as AI assumes responsibility for increasingly complex decisions.

The integration of AI with emerging technologies will further enhance defense capabilities. For example, quantum computing promises unprecedented computational power, allowing AI to analyze larger datasets more efficiently, identify complex attack patterns, and run simulations at speeds previously unimaginable. Similarly, advances in edge computing will enable AI to deploy predictive analytics and automated response closer to endpoints, reducing latency and improving the precision of real-time defenses. AI will also be instrumental in defending Internet-of-Things (IoT) ecosystems, autonomous vehicles, smart cities, and critical infrastructure, where decentralized and highly dynamic systems create unique security challenges.

Ethical and regulatory frameworks will evolve alongside AI capabilities. Autonomous systems will be capable of making decisions with real-world consequences, such as isolating devices, restricting access, or neutralizing potential threats. Guidelines, governance policies, and oversight mechanisms will be essential to ensure that these systems operate responsibly, maintain privacy, and comply with national and international standards. The future of AI cybersecurity will be defined not only by technical sophistication but also by the ability to balance security with trust, ethics, and societal expectations.

Ultimately, the future of AI-powered cyber defense will be characterized by intelligence, adaptability, and resilience. Organizations that implement these systems will enjoy unprecedented visibility into their networks, the ability to anticipate and neutralize threats, and the confidence of knowing that their digital assets are continuously protected. Cybersecurity will no longer be a reactive struggle; it will be a self-learning, self-improving discipline that evolves alongside attackers, closing gaps before they can be exploited. In this new era, survival will belong to those who embrace autonomous, intelligent defense, turning the digital battlefield into a space of resilience, foresight, and continuous improvement.

Adaptive AI will transform cybersecurity into a living, breathing ecosystem. Each attempted attack, whether successful or thwarted, will teach the system, strengthening its defenses and expanding its understanding of threats. Networks will become autonomous guardians, capable of defending themselves without human intervention in real time, yet guided by human oversight to ensure ethical, legal, and strategic alignment. This integration of intelligence, autonomy, and foresight represents the next frontier in cybersecurity—a frontier where AI is not just a tool but a true partner in protecting the digital world.

The coming years will see AI-driven defense systems that can operate globally, across cloud and edge infrastructure, endpoints, IoT devices, and interconnected networks. These systems will be adaptive, predictive, and self-healing, ensuring operational continuity, regulatory compliance, and resilience against threats that are faster, smarter, and more autonomous than ever before. In this future, AI is not just defending networks—it is shaping the very nature of cybersecurity, turning digital systems into intelligent, autonomous ecosystems capable of surviving and thriving in an increasingly hostile environment.

"The Day the AI Took Command"

The city slept under a blanket of quiet hums from data centers, cloud servers, and network hubs. To anyone walking the streets, nothing seemed unusual. But in the sprawling network of a multinational enterprise, an AI had taken command. It was autonomous, intelligent, and continuously learning. This system had observed thousands of devices, billions of transactions, and millions of user behaviors, creating a living map of the organization's digital environment. It knew normal patterns better than any human analyst and could detect even the smallest deviation instantly.

It started subtly. A minor anomaly in a remote endpoint—a login attempt from an unusual location—was immediately flagged. The AI analyzed behavioral patterns across devices, correlating the event with global threat intelligence. Within milliseconds, it determined that the activity was part of a coordinated intrusion attempting to infiltrate critical servers. Without alerting anyone, the AI isolated the device, redirected traffic, and began feeding false information to the attacker's tools. It was a silent war being waged entirely in code.

The intruders were sophisticated. They deployed polymorphic malware, AI-driven bots, and encrypted tunnels to bypass defenses. But every time they adapted, the AI adapted faster. It anticipated lateral movement, reinforced segmentation, and neutralized malware execution. Servers that had been targeted were automatically patched and restored from secure backups. Devices that had been compromised were quarantined, their operations restored in minutes. The AI's actions were flawless, faster than any human could react, and executed without error.

As the attack escalated, the AI began predictive simulations. It evaluated potential future moves of the intruders, tested defense scenarios internally, and deployed countermeasures preemptively. This proactive strategy ensured that even sophisticated attacks never reached critical systems. Every action was logged, analyzed, and incorporated into learning models, strengthening defenses for future incidents. The AI was teaching itself, evolving with every challenge, becoming smarter, faster, and more resilient.

Human operators arrived at the security operations center in the early hours, expecting chaos. Instead, they were greeted by dashboards displaying resolved anomalies, contained threats, and secure systems. The AI had acted autonomously, protecting data, ensuring continuity, and even preparing compliance reports for regulatory review. No alarms had gone off, no downtime had occurred, and the attackers were none the wiser. It was as if the network itself had grown consciousness, defending its digital territory with unparalleled intelligence.

By morning, the city awoke, unaware of the silent battle fought in its digital veins. The AI had not only stopped the intrusion—it had learned from it. Predictive models were updated, countermeasures refined, and the network's resilience improved. Each anomaly, each attempted exploit, had been transformed into knowledge, strengthening the defenses across the entire organization. Human teams now oversaw a system that was capable of thinking, adapting, and acting independently—a true autonomous guardian of the digital domain.

Mira, the lead analyst, leaned back and reflected on what she had witnessed. In the past, cybersecurity had been a reactive struggle, a race to respond to breaches and limit damage. Now, with adaptive, autonomous AI, the network itself had become the defender, the strategist, and the teacher. Each incident made the system stronger, and the organization was now protected in ways that were previously unimaginable. The AI had taken command, and it had done so with precision, foresight, and intelligence that ensured survival.

As sunlight poured into the operations center, Mira knew that this was only the beginning. Networks would continue to evolve, AI would become more intelligent, and cyber defense would transform into a living, self-learning ecosystem. Threats would come faster and smarter, but now, for the first time, the defenders had evolved faster. The AI had not only protected the digital world—it had ensured its resilience, autonomy, and future. And humanity, working in partnership with this intelligent guardian, was finally ahead of the curve.

Final Thoughts

As we conclude *AI-Powered Cyber Defense Systems*, it is important to reflect on the remarkable transformation that artificial intelligence has brought to cybersecurity. Over the past decade, the digital landscape has shifted from isolated networks and manual defenses to interconnected systems under constant threat from sophisticated adversaries. Attackers now deploy AI-driven malware, automated phishing campaigns, and deepfake impersonation, challenging traditional defenses at a scale and speed previously unimaginable. In response, AI-powered security systems have evolved from reactive tools into autonomous, adaptive guardians capable of protecting networks, endpoints, and cloud environments with intelligence and foresight that far surpasses human capacity. This book has explored the full spectrum of AI cybersecurity—from threat detection and behavioral analysis to automated response, predictive intelligence, and post-incident forensics—demonstrating that the future of defense lies in continuous learning, adaptability, and autonomy.

The most profound takeaway from this series is that cybersecurity is no longer simply a technical function; it is a strategic, organizational imperative. AI-powered defenses do more than block attacks—they analyze, predict, respond, and evolve, transforming the way organizations approach risk. Continuous monitoring allows networks to detect anomalies in real time, while adaptive models ensure that defenses improve with every incident. Automated response and self-healing infrastructure reduce downtime, prevent data loss, and maintain business continuity, while AI-driven analytics provide insights into risk management, compliance, and operational efficiency. Together, these capabilities create a comprehensive cybersecurity ecosystem where each component reinforces the others, resulting in a system that is greater than the sum of its parts.

Equally important is the human-AI partnership. While AI can process millions of events per second, isolate threats, and predict attack vectors, human expertise remains critical for oversight, strategy, and ethical decision-making. Security professionals guide AI deployment, evaluate high-risk scenarios, and ensure compliance with legal and regulatory frameworks. By leveraging AI to handle high-speed monitoring, threat hunting, and automated response, humans can focus on long-term planning, governance, and continuous improvement. This synergy between human judgment and artificial intelligence represents the future of resilient cybersecurity operations. Throughout this book, we have emphasized the transformative impact of AI on every layer of digital defense. At the endpoint, AI monitors device behavior, detects anomalies, and prevents lateral movement of threats. In cloud environments, AI maps dynamic workloads, secures data flows, and protects API endpoints. Within zero-trust architectures, AI continuously evaluates identities, permissions, and contextual risk, granting access only when behavioral patterns align with established norms. Predictive intelligence anticipates attacks, while post-incident forensics analyzes breaches to improve defenses continuously. Behavioral analysis uncovers threats invisible to traditional systems, and global threat intelligence sharing ensures that emerging threats are neutralized before they reach critical systems. These capabilities collectively create a network that is not only secure but self-aware, resilient, and capable of evolving in step with adversaries.

One of the most critical lessons is the importance of adaptability. Cyber threats are no longer static—they learn, adapt, and evolve in real time. Only defenses that learn at the same pace can remain effective. Adaptive AI models continuously update based on observed activity, threat intelligence, and incident outcomes, ensuring that the system becomes stronger with every encounter. Networks are no longer passive, waiting for attacks to occur—they are active participants in their own defense, learning from every anomaly, every breach attempt, and every suspicious pattern.

Another central theme is proactive defense. Traditional cybersecurity models often focus on reacting to attacks after they occur, a dangerous approach in a world of automated threats. AI transforms this paradigm, enabling organizations to anticipate attacks, implement preventive measures, and neutralize risks before they impact critical systems. By leveraging predictive analytics, behavioral monitoring, and scenario modeling, AI provides organizations with foresight that allows them to act before vulnerabilities are exploited. This proactive capability is essential in maintaining operational continuity and protecting critical assets in an increasingly hostile cyber environment.

Compliance and accountability are equally vital in modern cybersecurity. AI-powered analytics provide organizations with continuous monitoring and reporting capabilities, ensuring adherence to regulatory frameworks such as GDPR, HIPAA, CCPA, PCI-DSS, and NIST. Automated compliance reporting reduces administrative burden, streamlines audits, and provides verifiable evidence of security and governance measures. These capabilities reinforce trust with customers, partners, and regulators, demonstrating that organizations not only protect data but actively enforce policies that safeguard privacy, integrity, and operational resilience.

Finally, the future of cybersecurity is both challenging and promising. AI-driven attacks will continue to grow in sophistication, leveraging machine learning, automation, and global coordination. In response, defense systems must evolve toward autonomy, intelligence, and resilience. The next frontier includes self-healing networks, autonomous defense agents, predictive risk modeling, and seamless human-AI collaboration. Organizations that embrace these technologies will gain a decisive advantage, transforming cybersecurity from a defensive necessity into a strategic differentiator. They will be able to anticipate, neutralize, and learn from threats faster than adversaries can adapt, ensuring long-term resilience, operational continuity, and global trust.

In conclusion, AI-powered cyber defense is more than a set of tools; it is an ecosystem that integrates detection, response, learning, and governance into a unified, intelligent framework. Organizations that harness its potential will be equipped to survive and thrive in the face of unprecedented threats, ensuring that their digital assets, data, and operations remain secure. The journey explored in this book illustrates that in a world dominated by AI-driven attacks, the future belongs to those who can deploy, manage, and evolve intelligent defenses. The lessons, strategies, and insights presented here provide a roadmap for organizations seeking to navigate the complexities of modern cybersecurity, offering a foundation for resilient, adaptive, and autonomous protection in an increasingly digital world.

www.ingramcontent.com/pod-product-compliance
Lightning Source LLC
LaVergne TN
LVHW022015200926
848481LV00007B/2402